D1455049

found

PSALM 23

SALLY
LLOYD-JONES
AND JAGO

ZONDERKIDZ

Found

Copyright © 2007 by Sally Lloyd-Jones
Illustrations © 2017 by Jago

This edition ISBN: 978-0-310-76943-9

Requests for information should be addressed to:
Zonderkidz, 3900 *Sparks Drive SE, Grand Rapids, Michigan 49546*

All Scripture quotations, unless otherwise indicated, are taken from
The Holy Bible, New International Version®, NIV®. Copyright © 1973, 1978,
1984, 2011 by Biblica, Inc.® Used by permission. All rights reserved worldwide.

Zonderkidz is a trademark of Zondervan.

Design: Brooke Reynolds

Printed in China

19 20 21 22 23 /DSC/ 6 5 4 3 2 1

Dedication

For Harry, Olivia, Emily, Eleanor and Jonathan

Because the Fairy Tale really does come true!

SLJ

For my lovely family, the best

wife, daughter, and son in the world.

All the best,

Jago

God is my Shepherd.
And I am his little lamb.

He feeds me.

He guides me.

He looks after me.
I have everything I need.

Inside, my heart
is very quiet.

As quiet as lying still
in soft green grass
in a meadow
by a little stream.

Even when I walk through the
dark, scary, lonely places ...

I won't be afraid.

Because my Shepherd
knows where I am.

He is here with me.

He keeps me safe.
He rescues me.

He makes me strong
and brave.

He is getting wonderful
things ready for me.

Especially for me.

Everything I ever dreamed of!

He fills my heart
so full of happiness

I can't hold it all inside.

Wherever I go I know...

God's Never Stopping

Never Giving Up

Unbreaking

Always and Forever Love

will go, too!

PSALM 23

A psalm of David.

The LORD is my shepherd, I lack nothing.
   He makes me lie down in green pastures,
he leads me beside quiet waters,
   he refreshes my soul.
He guides me along the right paths
   for his name's sake.
 Even though I walk
   through the darkest valley,
I will fear no evil,
   for you are with me;
your rod and your staff,
   they comfort me.
You prepare a table before me
   in the presence of my enemies.
You anoint my head with oil;
   my cup overflows.
 Surely your goodness and love will follow me
   all the days of my life,
and I will dwell in the house of the LORD
   forever.